baking
mash-up

Victoria Glass

photography by
Clare Winfield

rps

LONDON • NEW YORK

For Joseph, Samuel & Sophie

Senior Designer Iona Hoyle
Commissioning Editor Stephanie Milner
Production Manager Gordana Simakovic
Art Director Leslie Harrington
Editorial Director Julia Charles

Food Stylist Maud Eden
Prop Stylist Jo Harris
Indexer Hilary Bird

First published in 2014
by Ryland Peters & Small
20–21 Jockey's Fields,
London WC1R 4BW
and
519 Broadway, 5th Floor
New York NY 10012
www.rylandpeters.com

10 9 8 7 6 5 4 3 2 1

Text © Victoria Glass 2014
Design and photographs © Ryland Peters
& Small 2014

ISBN: 978-1-84975-558-0

Printed and bound in China

A CIP record for this book is available from
the British Library.
US Library of Congress Cataloging-in-
Publication data has been applied for.

Acknowledgments

A big bear hug of thanks to my friends and
family for their sometimes brilliant, often
absurd and occasionally atrocious recipe
suggestions made during the writing of this
book. Most notably, Tom Wateracre,
Dolly Alderton, Stephen Gray, Lily Einhorn,
Helen Morant, Milli Taylor, Janet Bird,
Jane Ballantine, Susan Wilk, Jeff Turner,
Ylva Enström, Gina Navato and, last, but
certainly not least, my gorgeous boyfriend,
Richard Hurst. A couple of them even made
it into print.

A special thanks to Olivia Guest, my
wonderful agent, for looking after me so well
and for her continuing support. Thanks too
to my marvellous mum, for coming to the
rescue in the crumble cups trials when no
shop on earth seemed to be stocking rhubarb
(despite it being the height of the season).
Mum, your freezer really is a veritable
Aladdin's Cave of goodies.

A huge thank you to Stephanie Milner, my
fabulous editor, for all her patience, humour
and advice throughout the whole process of
writing. Heartfelt thanks must go to the
incredible team who turned my recipes and
ramblings into a beautiful book – that's
Clare Winfield on camera, Maud Eden on
ovens, Jo Harris on props and Iona Hoyle
on art directing. Thanks to the delightful
Lauren Wright, for her amazing publicity
know-how and to the lovely Julia Charles,
Leslie Harrington and Cindy Richards.

Finally, enormous thanks to all who helped
to eat their way through my mountain of test
bakes. You saved me from further damage
to my waistline and from committing the
cardinal sin of throwing perfectly good food
into the rubbish bin. Thank you. Thank you.

Notes

• Both British (Metric) and American
(Imperial plus US cups) are included in
these recipes for your convenience,
however it is important to work with one set
of measurements and not alternate between
the two within a recipe.

• Ovens should be preheated to the specified
temperatures. We recommend using an oven
thermometer. If using a fan-assisted oven,
adjust temperatures according to the
manufacturer's instructions.

• All spoon measurements are level unless
otherwise specified.

• All eggs are medium (UK) or large (US),
unless specified as large, in which case
US extra-large should be used. Uncooked
or partially cooked eggs should not be
served to the very old, frail, young children,
pregnant women or those with compromised
immune systems.

• Whenever the grated zest of citrus fruit is
called for within these recipes, buy unwaxed
fruit and wash well before using. If you
can only find treated fruit, scrub well in
warm soapy water before using.

• Whenever full-fat cream cheese is called
for within these recipes, it should be white,
creamy smooth and have at least 24 per
cent fat content, such as Kraft Philadelphia.

baking
mash-up

Contents

Introduction

Forget what your mother always told you, it's time to start playing with your food. Why stick solely with tradition, when you can make something original from something old? There's no need to ditch your favourite classics, but sometimes it's fun to try something new.

My baking mash-ups each combine two classic bakes to create something contemporary and playful. With pleasingly silly names, these delicious reinventions may not be suitable for the calorie-conscious, but are perfect for the adventurous baker looking for something novel to share with their loved ones.

These recipes also suit the indecisive amongst you. Why choose between cheesecake and brownies when you can smash them together to make chownies? No longer will you need to 'um' and 'ah' over Sachertorte or Lamingtons, now that Slamingtons have come into your life. The best of both worlds just got delicious.

Humpty Dumpty explains the unusual words in Jaberwocky to Alice in Lewis Carroll's *Through the Looking-glass* as, 'like a portmanteau – there are two meanings packed up into one word'. Similarly, these baking portmanteaus, pack two flavours as well as two meanings into one word, to create some tempting and exciting hybrids.

If naysayers take umbrage at my Frankenpastries, saying, 'if it ain't broke, don't fix it', let me direct them politely to the potato chip (or 'crisp' as my fellow Brits and I like to call them). Had it not been for a troublesome customer complaining that his fries were cut too thickly, George Crum, the chef at Moon's Lake House near Saratoga Springs, New York, may never have created our favourite portable salty snack in 1853. French fries still exist, but something new and exciting was born from them. Sometimes change can be good. And change needn't preclude the old.

Baking and eating are two of life's greatest pleasures and with the help of these mash-ups, you can crank your afternoons up a gear and impress your friends with these fun-filled teatime treats. Pull a Moonie out of your cake tin at them or offer up a Short baldi for them to dunk in their tea. You can dazzle them with your desserts by throwing a Wobbler on the table or covering it with Freckles. Whatever you decide to bake from this book, you can be sure your efforts won't be forgotten.

Toppings, sauces & fillings

The recipes in this book call for a variety of toppings, sauces and fillings all of which can be mixed and mashed in the different bakes in any way you like. You can of course buy many of these in pre-mixed or prepared packets but where's the fun in that? The smell of homemade chocolate fudge sauce flooding your kitchen is not only irresistible, but if you make it from scratch, you'll get to lick the bowl afterwards too.

Chocolate ganache topping

100 ml/scant ½ cup single/light cream
100 g/3½ oz. dark/bittersweet chocolate, chopped

Pour the cream into a saucepan or pot set over a low heat. Put the chopped chocolate in a heatproof bowl to the side. Once the cream scalds (you don't need to bring it to the boil), pour it over the chocolate and leave to stand for 1 minute. Stir the chocolate and cream together until all the chocolate has melted and you are left with a thick and glossy ganache. Set aside to cool before using as a topping.

Soured cream topping

180 ml/¾ cup soured cream
1 tablespoon caster/granulated sugar
2 teaspoons freshly squeezed lemon juice

Put the soured cream, lemon juice and sugar in a bowl and mix together to make the topping.

Sweet cream topping

300 ml/1¼ cups double/heavy cream
50 g/½ cup icing/confectioners' sugar
1 teaspoon pure vanilla extract

Whisk the cream until stiff but not dry. Sift over the icing/confectioners' sugar and mix in. Add the vanilla and whisk again.

Vanilla cream cheese topping

150 g/5 oz. (⅔ cup) cream cheese
50 g/3 tablespoons soft unsalted butter
300 g/2½ cups icing/confectioners' sugar
2 teaspoons pure vanilla extract
a splash of milk, if needed

Place the cream cheese and butter in a large bowl and beat together for about 30 seconds. Sift over half the icing/confectioners' sugar and whisk the mixture together. Sift over the remaining sugar and whisk for a good 2 minutes or until everything is thoroughly combined and fluffy. Whisk in the vanilla extract. You can add a splash of milk to slacken the mixture if necessary.

Chocolate fudge sauce

75 g/5 tablespoons unsalted butter
75 g/2½ oz. dark/bittersweet chocolate, broken into pieces
200 ml/¾ cup double/heavy cream
3 tablespoons golden/light corn syrup
1 teaspoon pure vanilla extract

To make the chocolate fudge sauce, place all the ingredients in a saucepan or pot set over a low heat and stir until the chocolate and butter have melted and all the ingredients have blended together to make a delicious sauce.

Sticky toffee sauce

75 g/5 tablespoons unsalted butter
1 x 397 g/14-oz. can sweetened condensed milk
75 g/⅓ cup dark muscovado sugar
2 teaspoons pure vanilla extract

Put the condensed milk, sugar, vanilla and the butter in a saucepan or pot set over a gentle heat. Stir until the butter has melted and the sugar has dissolved. Increase the heat and bring to the boil for a few minutes, stirring all the time, until thick and golden. Turn off the heat and leave the sauce in its pan until you're ready to drizzle some over your cake.

Sticky toffee buttercream

100 g/6½ tablespoons soft unsalted butter
200 g/1¾ cups icing/confectioners' sugar
2 teaspoons pure vanilla extract
3 tablespoons sticky toffee sauce (see following recipe)
a splash of whole milk, if needed

To make the sticky toffee buttercream, place the butter in a large bowl and whisk until soft and creamy. Sift over half the icing/confectioners' sugar and whisk again until combined. Sift over the remaining sugar and whisk for about 2 minutes. Add the toffee sauce and vanilla and whisk again. Whisk in a splash of milk to slacken the mixture if needed.

Place some clingfilm/plastic wrap over the bowl to prevent the top from crusting and set aside until needed.

Eton mess filling

300 ml/1¼ cups double/heavy or whipping cream
2 tablespoons icing/confectioners' sugar, sifted
400 g/14 oz. strawberries, washed and hulled

Purée half of the strawberries and pass them through a sieve/strainer to remove the seeds. Whip the cream and icing/confectioners' sugar together until stiff but not dry and fold in the strawberry purée. Slice the remaining strawberries and add them to the cream.

Marshmallows

sunflower oil, for greasing
1 tablespoon icing/confectioners' sugar
1 tablespoon cornflour/cornstarch
5 sheets of leaf gelatine
250 g/1¼ cups caster/granulated sugar
2 teaspoons liquid glucose
110 ml/scant ½ cup water
1 large egg white
1 teaspoon pure vanilla extract

a 20-cm/8-inch square pan, lightly oiled
a sugar thermometer

Sift together the icing/confectioners' sugar and cornflour/cornstarch and dust the prepared pan with a little of it.

Soak the leaf gelatine in the 75 ml/⅓ cup of cold water for at least 10 minutes to soften.

Place the sugar, glucose and water into a heavy-based saucepan or pot set over a medium heat. Stir the mixture with a wooden spoon until the sugar has dissolved. Stop stirring and bring to the boil. Place a sugar thermometer into the mixture and keep the syrup at a rolling boil until it reaches the hard-ball stage (122–127°C/252°–260°F). Remove the pan from the heat immediately. Squeeze the excess water out of the gelatine and melt it with 1 tablespoon of hot water before quickly stirring into the hot syrup.

Using a handheld electric whisk, whisk the egg white until very stiff and then slowly add the hot syrup, continuing to whisk on low speed all the time. The mixture will become thick and shiny. Add the vanilla and continue to whisk for 5–6 minutes or until the mixture is stiff enough to hold its shape.

Scrape the mixture into the prepared pan and level the top with a wet palette knife. Leave to set in a cool, dark place for at least 1 hour. Dust a chopping board with more of the icing/confectioners' sugar and cornflour/cornstarch and upturn the marshmallow pan onto it. If the marshmallow will not come out, slide an oiled knife round the sides of the pan before upturning again. Oil a sharp knife cut the marshmallow into 5-cm/2-inch squares. Dust the marshmallows in the icing/confectioners' sugar and cornflour/cornstarch.

Stollen meets vol-au-vent in this delightfully named confection.
Dainty morsels of puff pastry are filled with the spiced marzipan flavours
of Christmas stollen. These make the perfect sweet festive canapé.

Stoll-au-vents

300 g/10 oz. all-butter puff
pastry/dough

1 egg yolk beaten together with
1 tablespoon whole milk and a
pinch of salt, to glaze

For the marzipan filling
65 g/generous ½ cup
icing/confectioners' sugar, sifted

65 g/⅓ cup caster/granulated sugar

125 g/scant 1 cup ground almonds

50 g/⅓ cup (Zante) currants

25 g/¼ cup natural glacé cherries,
finely chopped

finely grated zest from ½ lemon

finely grated zest from ½ orange

1 teaspoon ground cinnamon

1 egg, lightly beaten

2 teaspoons lemon juice

a few drops of almond extract

1 teaspoon brandy

flaked/slivered almonds, to decorate

2 x baking sheets, greased and lined
with baking parchment

Makes 20

Preheat the oven to 200°C (375°F) Gas 5.

Roll the puff pastry/dough into a rectangle about the thickness of a one-pound/silver dollar coin and, using a pizza wheel or a sharp knife, cut 2 x 5-cm/2-inch squares. Use a small sharp knife to score a deep inner square on each piece of pastry/dough, so that each square has a scored edge of about 5 mm/¼ inch wide. Place the pastry squares on the baking sheets, a small distance apart. Brush the squares with the egg glaze and bake in the preheated oven for 10–12 minutes, or until risen and golden-brown. When ready, remove the squares from the oven and allow to cool. Using a knife, dig out any raw pastry from the centre of the square and discard.

Reduce the oven temperature to 180°C (350°F) Gas 4.

To make the marzipan filling, place the icing/confectioners' sugar, caster/granulated sugar and ground almonds in a mixing bowl and stir together. Mix in the currants, cherries, zest and cinnamon before making a well in the centre. Add the egg, lemon juice, almond extract and brandy and mix together with a fork until everything is well combined.

Place a marble-sized blob of the marzipan filling in the middle of each vol-au-vent square case and flatten. Lightly press a flaked/slivered almond or two into the marzipan filling and bake for 10 minutes, or until golden. Use a palette knife to transfer the stoll-au-vents to a wire rack to cool.

PASTRIES & TARTS

Half croissant half pretzel, these Franken-pastries offer the best of both worlds. Intensely buttery, flaky pastry beneath a crisp and salty shell.

Pretzant

325 g/2½ cups strong white/bread flour, sifted, plus extra to dust

1 teaspoon salt

35 g/2½ tablespoons caster/granulated sugar

1 x 7-g/¼-oz. sachet of fast-acting dried yeast

1 tablespoon malt extract

175 ml/¾ cup warm water

250 g/2 sticks unsalted butter, chilled

1 tablespoon bicarbonate of/baking soda

To garnish

sesame seeds

poppy seeds

sea salt

a baking sheet, greased and lined with baking parchment

Makes about 15

Put the flour into a large mixing bowl, then put the salt on one side of the bowl and the sugar and yeast on the other. In a separate bowl, stir the malt extract into the warm water. Pour half of the wet mixture into the dry. Mix together, adding a little of the wet mixture at a time, until fully combined. Tip the mixture out onto a lightly floured surface and knead for a few minutes until the dough is elastic. Put the dough back in the mixing bowl, cover with clingfilm/plastic wrap and put in the fridge for 1 hour.

Roll the dough out on a lightly floured surface to a rectangle about 20 x 40 cm/8 x 16 inches. Put the butter between two pieces of baking parchment and bash it with a rolling pin until you have a flat rectangle about 1-cm/½-inch thick. Place the butter in the centre of the rolled dough and fold the overhanging dough over the butter to form a parcel. Wrap in clingfilm/plastic wrap and return to the fridge for 30 minutes.

Roll the dough out a second time on a lightly floured surface to a rectangle about 20 x 40 cm/8 x 16 inches. Position the dough so that one of the narrow ends is facing you. Brush off any excess flour and fold the dough in thirds. Fold the section furthest away from you towards the middle and then fold the bottom section up to cover it. Press the edges together with your fingers. Turn the dough 90° so that the folds run vertically in front of you. Roll the dough once again into a neat rectangle 20 x 40 cm/8 x 16 inches in size. Brush off any excess flour and fold in three again, just as before. Seal the edges with your fingers and wrap the dough in clingfilm/plastic wrap and pop it back in the fridge for 1 hour to rest. Repeat the rolling, folding and resting two more times, then wrap the dough in clingfilm/plastic wrap and set in the fridge to rest for a few hours.

Roll the dough out a final time until it is 3 mm/⅛ inch thick. Cut the rolled dough into isosceles triangles approximately 20 x 10 cm/8 x 4 inches. With the narrow point of the triangle facing away from you, roll up the base towards it and place on the prepared baking sheet. Repeat with the remaining triangles, then set aside for 1 hour to rise.

Preheat the oven to 200°C (400°F) Gas 6.

Stir the bicarbonate of/baking soda into a large pot of boiling water. Drop the pretzants into the water, a few at a time, for a few seconds before removing them carefully with a slotted spoon. Place them on the remaining baking sheets and sprinkle with the seeds and salt. Bake for 15–20 minutes, then transfer the pretzants to a wire rack to cool completely before serving.

Eton Mess: strawberries, meringue and cream – what's not to like? Éclairs: choux/cream puff pastry filled with cream and covered in chocolate – what's not to like? Stick them together and the Eton Mess Éclair is born and, frankly, you'd have to be a lunatic not to want in on some of that action.

Eton mess éclairs

For the Eton mess meringues
2 egg whites
100g/½ cup caster/superfine sugar

For the éclair pastry/dough
150 ml/⅔ cup water (you can use half and half water and milk, if you prefer)
75 g/5 tablespoons butter, cubed
100 g/¾ cup plain/all-purpose flour
a pinch of salt
3 large eggs, beaten

Eton Mess Filling (page 9)

For the chocolate glaze
70 g/2½ oz. dark/bittersweet chocolate, broken in to pieces
1 tablespoon whole milk
1 tablespoon icing/confectioners' sugar

3 x baking sheets, greased and lined with baking parchment

a piping bag fitted with a large plain nozzle/tip

Makes 12
or 24 mini eclairs

Preheat the oven to 150°C (300°F) Gas 2.

To make the meringues, whisk the egg whites until they form stiff peaks and then, gradually, whisk in the caster/superfine sugar until it's all fully incorporated and you have a beautifully shiny and billowing meringue. Using a tablespoon, dollop rounded mounds of the meringue mixture onto one of the baking sheets. Put in the oven and immediately turn the temperature down to 140°C (275°F) Gas 1. Bake for 1 hour then turn the oven off. Leave the meringues in the oven until it is completely cold.

Preheat the oven to 220°C (425°F) Gas 7.

To make the éclair puff pastry/dough, put the water (or water and milk) in a saucepan or pot with the butter over a medium heat. Stir until the butter has melted, increase the heat and bring to a rolling boil, then immediately remove from the heat. Sift over the flour and salt and beat vigorously until the mixture comes together. Place the pan back over a gentle heat, stirring for 1 minute. Remove from the heat and leave to cool for 5 minutes. Using a wooden spoon, add a little of the egg at a time, beating well in between each addition. You may not need all of the egg. You are aiming for a soft, silky and shiny batter with a dropping consistency. Place the mixture in a large plastic piping bag fitted with a large plain nozzle/tip. Pipe 12 pastry/dough lines, each about 15 cm/6 inches long, onto the other baking sheets. Use a butter knife dipped in water to stop the mixture coming out. Bake for 20–25 minutes, or until the éclairs have puffed up and turned golden. Remove from the oven and stab the base of each bun with a skewer to allow the steam to escape. Return to the baking sheet and put them back in the oven for 5 minutes. Turn the oven off and open the door and leave the éclairs in there for another 5 minutes before transferring to a wire rack to cool.

Crumble the meringues over the Eton mess filling and fold into the mixture. Once the éclairs are cold, make a slice in the side of each éclair and fill with the Eton Mess. To make the chocolate glaze, melt the chocolate and the milk together in a heatproof bowl suspended over a pan of barely simmering water. Once the chocolate has melted, whisk in the icing/confectioners' sugar. Dip or spread each éclair with the chocolate glaze and leave to set before serving.

Oliver Cromwell banned Eccles cakes in 1653 because of their frivolity. This version goes one step further with an extra layer of frangipane.

Freckles cakes

For the flaky pastry/dough
800 g/6 cups plain/all-purpose flour, sifted, plus extra for dusting

1 teaspoon salt

500 g/4 sticks unsalted butter, chilled and cut into small cubes

freshly squeezed juice of 1 lemon

300 ml/1¼ cups fridge-cold water

For the currant filling
65 g/½ stick unsalted butter

180 g/1 cup (Zante) currants

135 g/⅔ cup light muscovado sugar

1 teaspoon ground cinnamon

½ teaspoon grated nutmeg

¼ teaspoon ground cloves

finely grated zest and freshly squeezed juice of 1 lemon

finely grated zest from 1 orange

For the frangipane
30 g/2 tablespoons unsalted butter, softened

30 g/2½ tablespoons caster/granulated sugar

1 small egg, beaten

15 g/2 tablespoons plain/all-purpose flour

20 g/2 tablespoons ground almonds

1 vanilla pod/bean

1 egg, beaten together with 2–3 tablespoons milk, to glaze

2 tablespoons demerara/turbinado sugar, to sprinkle

a 10-cm/2½-inch cookie cutter

2 x baking sheets, greased and lined with baking parchment

Makes 10

Begin by making the pastry/dough. Put the flour and salt into a large mixing bowl. Rub half of the butter into the flour with your fingertips until it resembles fine breadcrumbs. Add the lemon juice and two thirds of the water and using a fork, bring the mixture together into a dough. You may need to add more water, depending on the absorbency of the flour. Tip the dough out onto a lightly floured surface and roll it into a rectangle of roughly 30 x 40 cm/12 x 16 inches. Dot the remaining butter over the dough and fold the two ends into the middle and then in half. Wrap the pastry in clingfilm/plastic wrap and rest it in the fridge for 15 minutes, before repeating the rolling, folding and resting 3 more times. Wrap again and rest in the fridge for at least 45 minutes before using.

To make the currant filling, place all the ingredients in a saucepan or pot set over a medium heat and stir until the butter has melted. Bring the mixture to the boil until slightly thickened then remove from the heat and set aside to cool.

To make the frangipane, cream together the butter and sugar until pale and fluffy. Split the vanilla bean/pod in half lengthwise and scrape out the seeds. Gradually whisk in the beaten egg, followed by the flour, ground almonds and vanilla seeds. Chill the frangipane in the fridge for at least 30 minutes before using.

Preheat the oven to 200°C (400°F) Gas 6.

Roll the pastry out on a lightly floured surface to the thickness of about 3 mm/⅛ inch. Use the cookie cutter to stamp out 20 discs. Do not be tempted to twist the cutter, as it may affect the rise of your freckles cakes. Place a generous teaspoon of frangipane in the centre of 10 discs, followed by a tablespoon of the currant filling. Brush the edges of the discs with beaten egg and place a second disc over the top. Gently press the edges together to seal. Make three slashes across the top of each freckles cake with the tip of a sharp knife.

Transfer each freckles cake to the prepared baking sheets. Whisk together the egg and milk to make the glaze and brush the top of each cake. Sprinkle over some demerara/turbinado sugar and put them in the oven to bake for 20–25 minutes, or until the cakes are golden and have risen.

Transfer them to a wire rack to cool completely before serving.

A lightly spiced and chewy Florentine case filled with rich chocolate ganache; this chocolate tart/Florentine mash-up has decadent dinner party written all over it. Impress your friends with this impressive dessert, but be warned, they'll be hankering after a second invitation all too soon.

Florentart

Florentine tart case

40 g/3 tablespoons unsalted butter

85 ml/$\frac{1}{3}$ cup double/heavy cream

100 g/$\frac{1}{2}$ cup light muscovado sugar

1$\frac{1}{2}$ tablespoons clear honey

40 g/$\frac{1}{4}$ cup glacé cherries, chopped

115 g/1 scant cup desiccated/dried shredded coconut

100 g/$\frac{2}{3}$ cups flaked/slivered almonds

50 g/1$\frac{1}{2}$-inch piece stem ginger, finely chopped

40 g/$\frac{1}{4}$ cup mixed/candied peel

40 g/$\frac{1}{3}$ cup plain/all-purpose flour, sifted

a pinch of salt

100 g/3$\frac{1}{2}$ oz. melted dark/bittersweet chocolate

Filling

150 g/5 oz. dark/bittersweet chocolate, broken into pieces

75 g/5 tablespoons unsalted butter

300 ml/1$\frac{1}{4}$ cups double/heavy cream

60 g/5 tablespoons light muscovado sugar

1 vanilla pod/bean, split in half lengthwise and seeds scraped out

a pinch of salt

3 egg yolks

10 x 10-cm/4-inch individual tart pans with loose bottoms, buttered and floured

Makes 10

Preheat the oven to 180°C (350°F) Gas 4.

To make the Florentine tart case, put the butter, cream, sugar and honey in a saucepan or pot set over a gentle heat. Stir until the sugar has dissolved and then bring to the boil. Remove the pan from the heat and vigorously stir in the remaining ingredients. Leave the mixture to cool for a few minutes.

Use the back of a spoon to spread the mixture into each tart pan. Line each with crumpled parchment paper and baking beans. Bake for 8–10 minutes in the preheated oven. Remove the parchment and baking beans and continue to bake the tart cases in the oven for a few minutes longer until golden. Leave to cool to room temperature on a wire cooling rack, before easing the Florentine tart cases out of their pans, by pushing up the loose bottoms. This can be a little tricky, so you may have to warm the edges of the tart case with your hands to help them slide out more easily.

When the cases are cool, paint the insides with melted dark/bittersweet chocolate and let dry while you prepare the filling.

Put the chocolate in a heatproof bowl with the butter. Stir the cream and sugar together in a saucepan or pot set over a gentle heat until the sugar has completely dissolved. Increase the heat and once the cream begins to scald, pour it over the chocolate and butter. Leave for a minute, then mix together until the chocolate and butter have melted and the mixture is smooth and glossy. Stir in the vanilla and salt and whisk in the egg yolks. Pour the mixture into the Florentine tart cases and leave to set for at least 4 hours in the fridge.

Tarte Tatin and a torte get the hybrid treatment here. Tortes are cakes made without flour, often with ground nuts. Here, I've used ground almonds for a torte base topped with the buttery caramel apples of the classic tarte tatin. Irresistible.

Torte tatin

For the caramel apples

175 g/¾ cup plus 2 tablespoons caster/granulated sugar

1 teaspoon white wine or cider vinegar

40 ml/3 tablespoons water

40 g/3 tablespoons unsalted butter

a pinch of salt

4–5 medium apples, such as Cox, Bramley or Granny Smiths, peeled, cored and sliced into eighths

For the torte

4 eggs, separated

a pinch of salt

200 g/1 cup caster/granulated sugar

75 g/½ cup ground almonds

1 vanilla pod/bean, split in half lengthwise and seeds scraped out

a 22-cm/9-inch round deep cake pan, buttered

Serves 8

Put the sugar, vinegar and water into the cake pan and leave to soak for a couple of minutes. Place the cake pan over a gentle heat until all the sugar has dissolved and then turn the heat up a little and leave the syrup to simmer until it has become a pale golden caramel. Take the cake pan off the heat using oven gloves and stir in the butter and salt until well combined. Arrange the apple slices in the cake pan in concentric circles – be careful as the caramel will be very hot! Put the cake pan back on the heat and simmer for a few minutes. Take it off the heat and leave to cool completely.

Preheat the oven to 180°C (350°F) Gas 4.

To make the torte, whisk together the egg whites and salt until stiff but not dry and set aside. In a separate bowl, whisk together the egg yolks and sugar (no need to wash the whisk from the egg whites first) until pale and fluffy – this may take a few minutes with an electric whisk, so be patient. Fold in the almonds and the vanilla seeds until fully combined, before folding the egg whites into the mixture with a large metal spoon, using a slicing action to help prevent knocking the air out of the mixture. Pour the torte batter over the cold apples and bake for 25–30 minutes, or until an inserted skewer comes out clean. Leave to cool in the pan for about 5–10 minutes, before sliding a knife around the edge of the cake and, being careful not to burn yourself on the hot caramel, upturning onto a serving plate. The torte should be a rich golden brown as the caramel will have continued to cook in the oven.

Serve warm with crème fraîche or vanilla ice cream.

Cake meets pastry in these sinfully moreish treats. If a brownie inside a tart case wasn't enough already, I have added the warmth and zing of ginger and fresh orange zest. Short, crumbly pastry with a chewy, gooey brownie inside, you'll never have to choose between cakes or tarts again.

Tawnies

For the shortcrust pastry/dough

100 g/6½ tablespoons butter

80 g/⅔ cup icing/confectioners' sugar

a small pinch of salt

210 g/1⅔ cups plain/all-purpose flour

1 vanilla pod/bean, split in half lengthwise and seeds scraped out

2 egg yolks

1 tablespoon cold whole milk

For the brownie filling

150 g/5 oz. dark/bittersweet chocolate, roughly chopped

75 g/5 tablespoons unsalted butter

150 g/¾ cup light muscovado sugar

2 eggs, beaten

2 balls of Chinese stem ginger, finely chopped

finely grated zest from 1 orange

a pinch of salt

55 g/scant ½ cup rice flour

½ teaspoon baking powder

1 teaspoon ground ginger

8 x 10-cm/4-inch individual tart pans

Makes 8

To make the pastry/dough, cream together the butter, icing/confectioners' sugar and salt before rubbing in the flour, salt, vanilla seeds and egg yolks – you can do this by hand or in a food processor. When the mixture looks like coarse breadcrumbs, add the milk. Work the mixture gently until you have formed a dough. Wrap the dough in clingfilm/plastic wrap and pop it in the fridge for 1 hour.

Preheat the oven to 180°C (350°F) Gas 4.

Roll the pastry between two sheets of clingfilm/plastic wrap (this will prevent you from needing to use excess flour) to the thickness of 3 mm/⅛ inch and line the tart pans with it. Prick the pastry bases with a fork, and line with baking parchment and baking beans. Bake for 5–10 minutes, making sure the pastry edges don't brown too quickly. Remove the paper and baking beans and bake for another 5 minutes, or until the base is lightly golden. Leave the tart cases on a wire rack to cool.

To make the brownie filling, place the chocolate and butter in a heatproof bowl suspended over a pan of barely simmering water. Stir every now and then until the chocolate and butter have melted. Stir in the sugar and remove the bowl from the heat. Whisk in the beaten eggs, stem ginger and orange zest, before sifting over the salt, rice flour, baking powder and ground ginger. Fold in until fully combined and divide the mixture between the pastry cases.

Bake for 5 minutes, before turning the oven down to 140°C (275°F) Gas 1 and bake for a further 5–7 minutes. Leave to cool slightly before removing the tawnies from their pans.

BROWNIES & BARS

Two very special British tray bakes merged into one, my millionaire's flapjacks combine the buttery, syrup-drenched oats of flapjacks with the caramel and chocolate topping of millionaire's shortbread. Sticky and sweet, with a pleasing chewiness, this mash-up is extremely moreish. Consider yourself warned.

Millionaire jacks

For the flapjack base

150 g/¾ cup light muscovado sugar

150 g/10 tablespoons soft, unsalted butter

2 tablespoons golden/light corn syrup

200 g/1½ cups rolled porridge oats

a pinch of salt

For the caramel topping

125 g/1 stick unsalted butter

75 g/⅓ cup light muscovado sugar

25 g/2 tablespoons golden/light corn syrup

1 tablespoon pure vanilla extract

a pinch of salt

1 x 397-g/14-oz. can sweetened condensed milk

200 g/6½ oz. dark/bittersweet chocolate, broken into pieces

a 20-cm/8-inch loose-bottomed square cake pan, greased and lined with baking parchment

Makes 8 bars or 16 squares

Preheat the oven to 150°C (300°F) Gas 2.

Melt together the sugar, butter and golden/corn syrup over a gentle heat, stirring all the time. Take the pan off the heat and stir in the rolled porridge oats and salt until fully combined and coated.

Spoon the flapjack mixture into the prepared pan and press it level with the back of a spoon. Bake for 35–40 minutes. Leave to cool in the pan on top of a wire rack.

Meanwhile, make the caramel topping. Place all the ingredients, except the sweetened condensed milk, into a saucepan or pot and stir over a gentle heat until the butter has melted and the sugar has dissolved. Add the condensed milk and increase the heat, stirring frequently, and being careful not to let the base of the mixture catch. Bring to the boil, still stirring every now and then, until the mixture has thickened and turned a deep golden colour. Take the pan off the heat and leave to cool slightly.

Pour the warm caramel over the cooled flapjack base and leave to cool completely.

Place the chocolate in a heatproof bowl suspended over a pan of barely simmering water to melt. Stir every now and then. Once melted, leave to cool slightly before pouring the chocolate over the cold caramel. Leave to cool completely before pushing the base of the pan out and cutting the millionaires' flapjack into 8 bars (alternatively, for smaller portions, you can cut into 16 squares).

A cheesecake mixed with a brownie is even more gluttonously glorious than it sounds. Dark and gooey chocolate cake swirled with creamy vanilla-scented mascarpone; these chownies may make you think twice about bothering to bake anything else again.

Chownies

For the brownie mixture
300 g/10 oz. dark/bittersweet chocolate, broken into small pieces
100 g/3½ oz. milk/semisweet chocolate, broken into small pieces
200 g/14 tablespoons unsalted butter
400 g/2 cups light muscovado sugar
6 eggs, beaten
150 g/1¼ cups rice flour, sifted
½ teaspoon salt

For the cheesecake mixture
400 g/⅔ cup mascarpone
2 egg yolks
150 g/¾ cup caster/granulated sugar
2 teaspoons pure vanilla extract

a 25 x 20-cm/10 x 8-inch rectangular cake pan, greased and lined with baking parchment

Makes 16 squares

Preheat the oven to 180°C (350°F) Gas 4.

For the brownie mixture, place the chocolate and butter in a heatproof bowl suspended over a pan of barely simmering water. Stir until everything has melted and stir in the sugar. Take the bowl off the pan and whisk in the eggs, followed by the rice flour and salt. Pour the batter into the prepared cake pan and level it flat with a palette knife.

Vigorously beat the cheesecake ingredients together until smooth. Drop spoonfuls of the mixture over the brownie and use a skewer to swirl the two mixtures together into a marbled pattern. Bake for 45–55 minutes or until just set. If you insert a skewer it should come out still a little sticky. Cool in the pan on top of a wire rack for 20 minutes before turning out.

Cut into 16 squares and serve warm or cold.

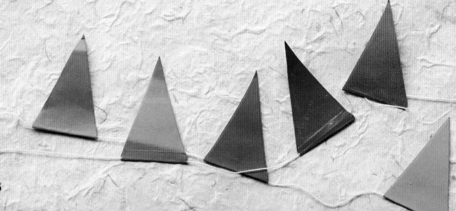

A mash-up between mousse and brownie, these moonies offer so much more than just a silly name. Rich and silky chocolate mousse sandwiched between two layers of sticky brownie; this mash-up will be sure to transform your afternoon cake fix from the mundane to the spectacular.

Moonies

For the brownies
250 g/8 oz. dark/bittersweet chocolate, broken into pieces
125 g/1 stick unsalted butter
¼ teaspoon salt
125 g/⅔ cup light muscovado sugar
125 g/⅔ cup caster/granulated sugar
4 eggs, beaten
75 g/⅔ cup rice flour
50 g/⅓ cup plus 1 tablespoon unsweetened cocoa powder
1 teaspoon baking powder

For the mousse filling
150 g/5 oz. dark/bittersweet chocolate, broken into pieces
55 g/½ cup icing/confectioners' sugar
100 g/6½ tablespoons unsalted butter
3 large eggs, separated
a pinch of salt
90 ml/⅓ cup plus 1 tablespoon double/heavy cream
a pinch of salt

2 x 20-cm/8-inch square cake pans, greased and lined with baking parchment

Makes 16 squares

Preheat the oven to 160°C (325°F) Gas 3.

To make the brownies, place the chocolate, butter and salt in a heatproof bowl suspended over a pan of barely simmering water. Once the chocolate and butter have melted, stir in the sugars. Remove the bowl from the heat and mix in the eggs. Sift over the flour, cocoa and baking powder and mix together. Divide the mixture between the prepared cake pans. Level the top with a palette knife and bake for 20–25 minutes. An inserted skewer should still have a little stickiness left on it. Leave to cool in the cake pans on top of a wire rack before turning out.

To make the mousse filling, melt the chocolate in a heatproof bowl suspended over a pan of barely simmering water. Once melted, take the chocolate off the heat and stir in the butter until melted. Whisk in the egg yolks, one at a time, until fully incorporated. Sift over the icing/confectioners' sugar and mix in. In a spotlessly clean bowl and with clean whisks, whisk the egg whites with the salt to stiff peaks. Set aside while you whisk the cream to stiff peaks – there's no need to wash up the whisks for the cream.

Fold the cream into the chocolate mixture. Next, fold in the egg whites using a large metal spoon. Place one of the cold brownies inside a deep cake pan (preferably with a loose-bottom) of the same size. Pour the mousse over the top and level it over. Finally, place the other brownie on top and put the cake pan in the fridge to chill for at least 8 hours (or overnight).

Run a knife around the edges of the cake pan, before taking the moonie out of its pan. Carefully slice into 16 squares.

A mash-up between two of Britain's favourite treats: the Garibaldi and shortbread. Garibaldi cookies have a layer of currants squashed between two very thin rectangles of cookie dough. I have simply swapped the cookies for buttery shortbread to make Short Baldis – they are excellent dunked in a cup of tea.

Short baldi

130 g/1 stick unsalted butter, softened
65 g/⅓ cup caster/granulated sugar
135 g/1 cup plain/all-purpose flour
50 g/⅓ cup rice flour
a pinch of salt
1 teaspoon pure vanilla extract
50 g/⅓ cup (Zante) currants
1 egg white, lightly beaten
1 tablespoon granulated/white sugar, to sprinkle

a baking sheet, greased and lined with baking parchment

Makes 16

Cream together the butter and sugar in a large bowl until light and fluffy. Sift over the flours and salt and mix together with the vanilla extract until just combined. Do not overwork the dough or the biscuits will be tough. Chill the dough for at least 30 minutes in the fridge.

Roll out the dough on a lightly floured surface to 1 cm/⅜ inch thick rectangle and sprinkle the currants over half the surface. Fold the other half on top and roll again into rectangle 5 mm/³⁄₁₆ inch thick. Trim the edges and cut the dough into 16 fingers. Transfer the cookies to the baking sheet and pop them in the fridge for 30 minutes to chill.

Preheat the oven to 170°C (325°F) Gas 3.

Brush the top of each cookie with a little egg white and sprinkle them with granulated sugar.

Bake for 12–15 minutes, before transferring on to a wire rack to cool completely.

Old-fashioned British Queen of Puddings meets modern cupcake in this hybrid. It takes the best bits of the pudding – jam, custard and crunchy meringue and sticks them in and on a cupcake. Pretty as a picture, whomever you make these treats for will want to be your friend for life.

Queen of cupcakes

For the crème pâtissière
2 egg yolks
30 g/2½ tablespoons caster/granulated sugar
15 g/2 tablespoons cornflour/cornstarch
175 ml/¾ cup whole milk
1 vanilla pod/bean

For the cakes
200 g/1 cup caster/granulated sugar
200 g/1 stick plus 5 tablespoons unsalted butter, softened
200 g/1⅔ cups self-raising/rising flour
1 teaspoon baking powder
4 eggs
a pinch of salt
finely grated zest from 1 lemon
a splash of whole milk, if needed
4 tablespoons raspberry jam/jelly

For the meringue topping
2 egg whites
a pinch of salt
100 g/½ cup caster/superfine sugar

a 12-hole muffin pan lined with paper cases/liners
a piping bag fitted with a large star nozzle/tip

Makes 12

Begin by making the crème pâtissière (this can be made the day before). Put the egg yolks and sugar in a heatproof bowl and whisk until pale and fluffy. Sift over the cornflour/cornstarch and whisk in. Split the vanilla pod/bean in half lengthwise and scrape out the seeds. Put the milk and vanilla in a saucepan or pot over a gentle heat and bring up to a simmer. Fish out the vanilla pod/bean and slowly pour the milk over the eggs, whisking as you do so. Decant the custard back into the saucepan and stir over a medium heat and bring to the boil. Once the custard is thick enough to dollop, pour it into a cold bowl or jug/pitcher and cover the top with clingfilm/plastic wrap to prevent a skin forming. Leave to cool to room temperature before putting it in the fridge.

Preheat the oven to 180°C (350°F) Gas 4.

To make the cakes, place all the cake ingredients into a large mixing bowl and whisk until light and fluffy. Whisk in a splash of milk if the batter is too stiff. Divide the mixture between the paper cases and bake for 20–25 minutes, or until an inserted skewer comes out clean. Transfer the cakes to a wire rack to cool.

Preheat the oven to 180°C (350°F) Gas 4.

Once cold, use a small, sharp knife to hollow out the centre of each cake. Drop a teaspoonful of jam/jelly into the cavity of each cake. Next, spoon a generous blob of crème pâtissière on top. Once all the cakes are filled place them on a baking sheet.

Make the meringue topping by whisking the egg whites with a pinch of salt until stiff, but not dry. Add the sugar, a little at a time, whisking on low speed between each addition. You should be left with a shiny, thick meringue. Transfer the meringue to a piping bag fitted with a large star nozzle/tip and pipe a generous swirl of meringue on to each cake. Pop the cakes back in the oven for 10–15 minutes, or until the meringue is slightly golden. Leave to cool again, before serving.

Tiramisù just got portable in this muffin mash-up. A fluffy muffin, soaked in espresso, filled with Marsala-spiked mascarpone and topped with a light dusting of cocoa. Tiramuffins make the ideal 'pick me up'.

Tiramuffins

For the cake
80 g/⅓ cup caster/granulated sugar

2 large eggs

80 g/⅔ cup plain/all-purpose flour

40 g/3 tablespoons soft, unsalted butter

1 vanilla pod/bean, split in half lengthwise and seeds scraped out

For the sweetened espresso
120 ml/½ cup (4 oz.) hot espresso

2 tablespoons dark rum

15 g/1 tablespoon caster/granulated sugar

For the mascarpone topping
3 eggs, separated

45 ml/3 tablespoons Marsala

185 g/¾ cup mascarpone

75 g/⅓ cup caster/superfine sugar

1 tablespoon unsweetened cocoa powder, for dusting

a 12-hole muffin pan lined with paper cases/liners

Makes 12

Preheat the oven to 180°C (350°F) Gas 4.

To make the cake, place the sugar and eggs in a heatproof bowl over a pan of gently simmering water. Use an electric whisk to beat until the mixture is hot. Remove the bowl from the heat and continue to whisk on high speed for about 10 minutes. The mixture should double in volume and be at the ribbon stage.

Melt the butter and add it to the side of the egg mixture bowl and whisk in to incorporate. Mix in the vanilla seeds. Sift the flour over the mixture and fold in using a large metal spoon. Be careful not to knock the air out of the batter.

Divide the batter between the paper cases/liners and bake in the preheated oven for 20 minutes, or until an inserted skewer comes out clean. Leave the cake to cool in the pan before turning out.

Use a small, sharp knife to cut inverted cone shapes out of the centre of each cake. Stir the rum and caster/granulated sugar into hot espresso until the sugar has dissolved. Brush each cake generously with the sweetened espresso.

To make the mascarpone topping, whisk the egg whites until stiff, but not dry. In a separate bowl, whisk the egg yolks and sugar until pale and fluffy. Whisk in the Marsala and stir in the mascarpone. Once fully incorporated, fold the whipped egg whites in with a large metal spoon. Pour the mascarpone topping onto each muffin until it reaches the top of the paper cases. Place the cakes in the fridge for at least 4 hours, or until set. In fact, they are best eaten the day after they're made. Dust the tops with cocoa and serve.

Tart rhubarb inside sweet cupcakes, with a crumble topping makes this mash up tick all the right boxes for the perfect afternoon indulgence. Rhubarb crumble has always been a favourite of mine, but apples, blackberries, plums or apricots will all make delicious alternatives.

Crumble cups

For the rhubarb
1 vanilla pod/bean, split in half lengthwise and seeds scraped out

finely grated zest from 1 small orange

40 g/3 tablespoons caster/granulated sugar

175 g/6 oz. rhubarb, diced

For the crumble topping
50 g/¼ cup light muscovado sugar

50 g/⅓ cup plus 1 tablespoon plain/all-purpose flour

25 g/3 tablespoons rolled porridge oats

25 g/2½ tablespoons ground almonds

1 vanilla pod/bean, split in half lengthwise and seeds scraped out

50 g/3 tablespoons unsalted butter, chilled and cut into small cubes

For the cupcakes
150 g/¾ cup light muscovado sugar

150 g/10 tablespoons unsalted butter, softened

3 eggs, beaten

100 g/¾ cup self-raising/rising flour

1 teaspoon baking powder

50 g/⅓ cup ground almonds

a pinch of salt

a 12-hole muffin pan lined with paper cases/liners

Makes 12

Preheat the oven to 150°C (300°F) Gas 2.

To prepare the rhubarb, stir the vanilla seeds and orange zest into the sugar in a large bowl and toss in the rhubarb. Leave to stand for 30 minutes before tipping onto a baking sheet and baking for 25–30 minutes, or until the rhubarb has softened, but still holds its shape. Leave to cool completely.

Preheat the oven to 180°C (350°F) Gas 4.

To make the crumble topping, place all of the ingredients except the butter in a food processor and blitz everything together. Add the butter and pulse until the mixture resembles breadcrumbs.

To make the cupcakes, cream together the light muscovado sugar and butter before slowly adding the egg, a little at a time. Sift over the flour and baking powder, add the ground almonds and salt and mix in until everything is completely combined. Fold in the cold rhubarb along with any cooking juices. Spoon the mixture into the muffin pan. Top each cake with a generous spoonful of the crumble topping and bake for 20–25 minutes, or until the crumble topping is golden and an inserted skewer comes out clean. Transfer the crumble cups to a wire rack to cool completely.

You'll never have to make the choice between cake and macaroons again, with these cute little macaroon-topped almond cupcakes. Pretty in pink, these dainty treats are aromatic with a dash of rose water and a subtle hint of lemon.

Cakeroons

For the macaroon top
2 egg whites
a pinch of salt
115 g/1 cup icing/confectioners' sugar
85 g/½ cup ground almonds
a little pink food dye (optional)

For the cake
175 g/¾ cup plus 2 tablespoons caster/granulated sugar
175 g/1½ sticks soft, unsalted butter
125 g/1 cup self-raising/rising flour, sifted
50 g/⅓ cup ground almonds
½ teaspoon baking powder
finely grated zest of 1 lemon
1 teaspoon rose water
3 eggs

fresh raspberries, to garnish

a 12-hole muffin pan lined with paper cases/liners

Makes 12

Preheat the oven to 180°C (350°F) Gas 4.

To make the macaroon top, whisk the egg whites and salt until stiff. Sift over the icing/confectioners' sugar and ground almonds and fold into the whites. Mix in a little pink food dye and transfer the mixture to a piping bag and leave to rest while you make the cakes.

Put all the cake ingredients in a large mixing bowl and whisk for a couple of minutes until well combined. Divide the cake batter between the paper cases and bake for 15 minutes.

Remove the cakes from the oven, snip off the end of the piping bag and squeeze out just enough of the macaroon mixture to cover the top of each cake. Lift the muffin pan and drop it on the table twice to get rid of any air bubbles and bake for a further 15 minutes. The tops seem generally less likely to crack if you don't use a fan oven.

Leave the cakeroons to cool before topping with a fresh raspberry and serving.

Austrian Sachertorte mashed with Australian Lamingtons. Slamingtons are an inviting combination of dark, close-textured chocolate cake, apricot jam/jelly, chocolate ganache and desiccated coconut. They look like lamingtons but hide a Sachertorte surprise inside.

Slamington

For the cake
200 g/6½ oz. dark/bittersweet chocolate, broken into pieces
6 large eggs, separated
200 g/1 cup caster/granulated sugar
150 g/1 cup ground almonds
½ teaspoon salt

For the chocolate icing
300 g/10 oz. dark/bittersweet chocolate, broken into pieces
200 ml/¾ cup whole milk
50 g/½ cup icing/confectioners' sugar, sifted

2–3 tablespoons apricot jam/jelly
225 g/3 cups shredded/desiccated coconut, to decorate

a 20-cm/8-inch square cake pan, greased and lined with baking parchment

Makes 16

Preheat the oven to 180°C (350°F) Gas 4.

Melt the chocolate in a heatproof bowl suspended over a pan of barely simmering water. Once melted, take the bowl off the heat and leave to cool slightly. In the meantime, whisk the egg yolks and sugar until pale and mousse-like. Whisk in the cooled melted chocolate and mix in the ground almonds. In a separate, spotlessly clean, bowl whisk the egg whites with the salt until stiff peaks form. Vigorously beat one-third of the egg whites into the chocolate mixture, before gently folding in the rest with a large metal spoon. Pour the mixture into the prepared pan and bake in the preheated oven for 30–35 minutes, or until an inserted skewer comes out clean. If the top is browning too quickly, you can cover it with foil halfway through the baking time. Leave the cake to cool completely in its pan on top of a wire rack before turning out.

Once cold, pop the cake in the fridge for half an hour to firm up. This will make cutting the cake into cubes easier.

Once chilled, cut the cake into 16 equal cubes.

Melt the jam/jelly and place each cube of cake on the end of a fork before dunking them in the jam until fully coated. Place the cubes of cake on a wire rack with a piece of baking parchment underneath to catch the drips. Once the jam has set, make the chocolate icing.

Melt the chocolate with the milk in a heatproof bowl over a pan of barely simmering water. Once melted, take off the heat and whisk in the icing/confectioners' sugar. Leave to cool slightly. Put the desiccated coconut in a bowl. Place a cube of cake on the end of a fork and dunk it into the chocolate icing. Make sure the cube is fully coated in icing and then roll it in the coconut. Place the cube of cake on a sheet of baking parchment to set. Repeat until all the cubes of cake are coated and leave to set.

Moist red velvet cake whoopie pies sandwiched together with vanilla cream cheese frosting. These colourful sweet treats are easy to make and even easier to eat. One is rarely enough...

Red velvet whoopie pies

For the whoopie pies

110 g/7 tablespoons unsalted butter, softened

150 g/¾ cup caster/granulated sugar

2 eggs

2 teaspoons pure vanilla extract

2 teaspoons red extra paste colour food dye

120 ml/½ cup buttermilk

220 g/1¾ cups plain/all-purpose flour

20 g/2½ tablespoons unsweetened cocoa powder

½ teaspoons baking powder

1 teaspoon cider vinegar

1 teaspoon bicarbonate of/baking soda

For the cream cheese filling

100 g/6½ tablespoons unsalted butter, softened

400 g/3⅓ cups icing/confectioners' sugar, sifted

2 teaspoons pure vanilla extract

150 g/5 oz. cream cheese, softened

2 x baking sheets, greased and lined with baking parchment

a large piping bag fitted with a plain nozzle/tip

Makes 15

Preheat the oven to 180°C (350°F) Gas 4.

Cream together the butter and sugar until light and fluffy. Beat in the eggs and the vanilla extract. Add food colouring into the buttermilk. Sift together the flour, cocoa and baking powder into a large bowl.

Mix half of the flour mixture into the butter mixture. Stir in half of the buttermilk. Repeat with the remaining flour mixture and buttermilk until just combined. Stir the vinegar into the bicarbonate of/baking soda and fold into the cake batter.

Spoon the mixture into a large piping bag fitted with a plain nozzle/tip. Pipe 30 even rounds (about 1 level tablespoon of batter) on to the prepared baking sheets, about 5 cm/2 inches apart, to allow room for spreading. Bake for 8–10 minutes or until the cakes spring back when gently pressed. Leave the cakes on the baking sheets for a few minutes before transferring them to a wire rack to cool completely.

To make the filling, whisk together the cream cheese and butter until smooth, before sifting over the icing/confectioners' sugar in two stages, whisking thoroughly between each addition. Whisk in the vanilla extract. Sandwich the red velvet whoopie pies together with a generous smear or piping of cream cheese filling and serve.

Buttery brioche meets glazed doughnut in this cheeky mash-up. A generous measure of bourbon adds an extra splash of bromance to these moreish treats.

Bronut

For the brioche dough

75 ml/⅓ cup warm (but not hot) milk

35 g/2½ tablespoons caster/granulated sugar

1 x 7-g/¼-oz. sachet of fast-acting dried yeast

500 g/4 cups strong white/bread flour, sifted

1 teaspoon salt

6 eggs, beaten

350 g/1½ sticks unsalted butter, softened

sunflower oil, for frying

cinnamon sugar, for rolling (optional)

For the bourbon glaze

375 g/3 cups icing/confectioners' sugar, sifted

3 tablespoons bourbon

a dough scraper

a large mixing bowl, oiled

a 7½-cm/3-inch round cookie cutter

a 2½-cm/1-inch round cookie cutter

2 x baking sheets, greased and lined with baking parchment

Makes 14–16

Begin by preparing the brioche dough. This is a very wet dough, so prepare to get messy. Combine the milk and sugar in a large mixing bowl or jug/pitcher and stir in the yeast. In a separate bowl mix together the flour and salt, then make a well in the middle. Pour in the beaten eggs and then the milk and yeast mixture. Use a butter knife to cut through the wet and dry ingredients to combine. Using one hand begin to knead the mixture in the bowl until fully combined. Tip the mixture out onto a lightly oiled surface and continue to knead using a dough scraper to prevent your dough from getting stuck to the work surface. It will take some time and effort, but persevere until there are no egg streaks. Alternatively, you can do all this more speedily in a free-standing mixer fitted with a dough hook.

Add the butter a little at a time. Knead thoroughly between each addition, then continue to knead the dough by lifting and slapping it on the work surface until the dough is smooth, shiny and elastic. Place the dough in the prepared, oiled bowl and cover with clingfilm/plastic wrap. Place the bowl in a warm place for at least an hour, or until the dough has doubled in volume. Knock back the dough and gently knead for a couple of minutes before covering again and putting in the fridge for 8 hours, or overnight.

Roll out the dough until it is about 2.5 cm/1 inch thick. Use the bigger cookie cutter to cut out as many rounds as you can. Then, use the smaller cutter to cut out the holes. Place the bronuts and removed holes on the prepared baking sheets and set aside to rise for 30–60 minutes.

Fill a wide, heavy-bottomed frying pan/skillet with 5 cm/2 inches of oil. Set over a medium–high heat until it reaches 180°C (350°F), or until a small piece of bread dropped into the oil sizzles and turns golden brown. Take care as if the oil is too cool, the bronut will be sodden with grease, but if the oil is too hot, the outside will cook before the inside. Use a slotted spoon to place a few bronuts carefully into the hot oil. After 2–3 minutes, flip the bronuts over and fry until they are golden on both sides. Lift the bronuts out of the oil with the slotted spoon and drain on paper towels. Repeat with the remaining bronuts and their holes too, if you wish. Leave to cool for 10–15 minutes before glazing. The holes are very nice simply rolled in cinnamon sugar, but they should be rolled immediately after frying.

To make the bourbon glaze, whisk the bourbon and 90 ml/⅓ cup water into the icing/confectioners' sugar until fully combined and you have a smooth and pourable consistency. Drizzle the bronuts with the glaze and enjoy!

Boston Cream Pie meets Brooklyn Blackout Cake in this East Coast baking mash-up. The vanilla-rich crème pâtissière filling shines a little lightness inside the dark blackout chocolate cake. The Boston chocolate glaze is sprinkled with Brooklyn's cake crumbs: a perfect pairing of two famous bakes.

Boston blackout cake

For the cake

250 g/2 sticks unsalted butter, softened

250 ml/1 cup whole milk

125 g/½ cup plus 2 tablespoons dark muscovado sugar

175 g/¾ cup plus 2 tablespoons caster/granulated sugar

3 eggs

150 g/1 cup plus 2½ tablespoons plain/all-purpose flour

100 g/¾ cup unsweetened cocoa powder

1 teaspoon bicarbonate of/ baking soda

½ teaspoon baking powder

¼ teaspoon salt

For the crème pâtissière

375 ml/1½ cups whole milk

2 vanilla pods/beans

2 whole eggs, plus 3 egg yolks

75 g/⅓ cup caster/superfine sugar

35 g cornflour/cornstarch, sifted

20 g/1 tablespoon plus 1 teaspoon unsalted butter, cut into small cubes

Chocolate Ganache Topping (page 8)

2 x 20-cm/8-inch round baking pans, greased and lined with baking parchment

Serves 8

Preheat the oven to 180°C (350°F) Gas 4.

To make the cake, put the butter, milk and dark muscovado sugar in a saucepan or pot set over a gentle heat and stir until the sugar and butter have melted. Whisk together the caster/granulated sugar and eggs in a large mixing bowl until light and fluffy. Continue to whisk, while gradually adding the hot butter mixture. Sift over the flour, cocoa, bicarbonate of soda/baking soda, baking powder and salt and whisk until fully combined. Divide the batter between the two prepared pans and bake for 20–25 minutes, or until an inserted skewer comes out clean. Leave the cakes to cool in their pans on a wire rack for 10 minutes before turning out on to the wire rack to cool completely.

To make the crème pâtissière, split the vanilla pods/beans lengthwise and scrape out the seeds. Put the milk and vanilla seeds and pods/beans in a saucepan or pot set over a gentle heat and simmer for 5 minutes. In the meantime, put the eggs, egg yolks, sugar and cornflour/cornstarch in a heatproof bowl and whisk together until pale and creamy. Place a sieve/strainer over the bowl to catch the vanilla pods/beans and pour the hot milk over the egg mixture. Whisk before transferring the mixture back to the pan. Stir continuously over a gentle heat for 1–2 minutes, before increasing the heat and bringing to the boil. Keep stirring the bubbling mixture until the crème pâtissière has thickened. Take the pan off the heat and vigorously whisk in the butter until it has melted. Transfer to a jug/bowl and cover in clingfilm/plastic wrap to prevent a skin forming. Once cool, transfer to the fridge.

Using a long serrated knife, carefully trim a little from the top of each cake to level their surfaces. Place the cake trimmings in a food processor and blitz into crumbs – this often works best if you have left the trimmings sitting around to get a little stale first.

Place one cake on a serving plate and spread the cold crème pâtissière very thickly on top – this cake demands a generous filling. Sandwich the other cake on top. Pour the slightly cooled chocolate ganache topping over the top of the cake. Use a palette knife to encourage it to spread to the edges if necessary. Sprinkle the top of the cake with the cake crumbs and leave to set for 20 minutes before serving.

CAKES & DESSERTS

This portmanteau bake combines the enduring appeal of pavlova with the sophisticated smoothness of blackcurrant bavarois. The tanginess of the blackcurrant cuts through the sweetness of the meringue beautifully, creating the perfect dessert for a special occasion.

Bavlova

For the pavlova

6 egg whites

a pinch of salt

335 g/1²/₃ cups caster/ superfine sugar

2 teaspoons cornflour/cornstarch

1 teaspoon white wine vinegar

1 vanilla pod/bean, split in half lengthwise and seeds scraped out

100 g/3 oz. melted white chocolate

For the bavarois

2 egg yolks

50 g/¼ cup caster/superfine sugar

125 ml/½ cup single/light cream

3 sheets of leaf gelatine

1 tablespoon hot water

1 egg white

100 ml/scant ½ cup double or whipping cream

175 ml/¾ cup blackcurrant or blackberry purée (made from 250 g/ 8 oz. blitzed blackcurrants/other seasonal berries passed through a sieve/strainer)

1 tablespoon crème de cassis

500 g/1 lb. mixed berries, to top

icing/confectioners' sugar, to dust

a baking sheet, greased and lined with baking parchment

Serves 8

Preheat the oven to 150°C (300°F) Gas 2.

To make the pavlova, whisk the egg whites with the salt in a large bowl, until stiff peaks form. Gradually, one spoonful at a time, add the sugar, whisking between each addition. The mixture should be thick and glossy. Whisk in the cornflour/cornstarch and vinegar before whisking in the vanilla. Spoon generous dollops of the mixture in a ring shape about 25 cm/10 inches in diameter on to the prepared baking sheet. Spoon more of the mixture in the middle and build up the sides higher, so that there is plenty of room in the middle to be filled with bavarois later. Put in the oven and immediately reduce the temperature to 140°C (275°F) Gas 1. Bake for 1 hour.

Turn the oven off, but leave the pavlova inside, with the oven door shut, until the oven is cold. It's easiest to make this stage in the evening and leave in the oven overnight to cool.

In the meantime, make the bavarois. Whisk the egg yolks and caster/superfine sugar together in a heatproof bowl. Place the cream in a saucepan or pot and heat until it begins to boil. Whisk the hot cream in the egg mixture before tipping the custard back into the pan and stir until the custard has slightly thickened. Decant the custard into a cold jug/pitcher and stir the blackcurrant puree and crème de cassis into the custard. Leave to cool completely before transferring to the fridge – you can leave this in the fridge overnight while the pavlova slowly cools in the oven. Once the pavlova is completely cold, paint the inside with the cooled melted white chocolate. This will provide a delicious seal to prevent the bavarois from seeping through the meringue.

Soak the leaf gelatine in cold water for 10 minutes to soften. Squeeze the cold water out of the gelatine and melt it with the hot water. Whisk the melted gelatine into the blackcurrant bavarois. In a spotlessly clean bowl, whisk the egg whites until stiff but not dry. In a separate bowl, but with the same whisk (no need to wash it up), whisk the cream and fold it into the blackcurrant custard until fully combined. Finally, fold in the whipped egg whites until fully combined. Carefully pour the bavarois in the middle dip of the pavlova and pop it in the fridge to set for at least 6 hours, or overnight. Once set, top with berries, dust with icing/confectioners' sugar and serve.

Rest assured, this cinnamon cheesecake will not pack you off to bed with a cold. Instead, this baked cheesecake has a delicious twist in the form of a snickerdoodle base. A buttery cinnamon cookie crust meets a velvety smooth and indulgent filling.

Sneezecake

For the snickerdoodle base
60 g/5 tablespoons unsalted butter

80 g/⅓ cup caster/granulated sugar

1 small egg, beaten

95 g/¾ cup plain/all-purpose flour

½ teaspoon cream of tartar

½ teaspoon baking powder

a pinch of salt

1 tablespoon caster/granulated sugar

1 teaspoon ground cinnamon

For the filling
725 g/24 oz. full fat Philadelphia cream cheese

200 g/1 cup caster/granulated sugar

a pinch of salt

25 g/3 tablespoons cornflour/cornstarch

2 vanilla pods/beans, split in half lengthwise and seeds scraped out

1 teaspoon ground cinnamon

finely grated zest from 1 lemon

2 teaspoon freshly squeezed lemon juice

3 eggs, plus 1 yolk

160 ml/⅔ cup soured cream

Soured Cream Topping (page 8)

a 20-cm/8-inch deep loose-bottomed round cake pan, greased and lined with baking parchment

Serves 8

Preheat the oven to 200°C (375°F) Gas 5.

To make the snickerdoodle base, cream the butter and sugar together until pale and fluffy. Gradually whisk in the egg and sift over the flour, cream of tartar, baking powder and salt. Mix all the ingredients until they come together to form a dough. Put the dough in the fridge to chill for 30 minutes or until firm. Roll out the dough into a 20-cm/8-inch round. Mix the caster/granulated sugar and cinnamon together and liberally coat the top of the dough with half of it. Turn it upside down and press it gently into the pan base, so the cinnamon sugar is underneath. Liberally coat the other side of the snickerdoodle dough with the rest of the cinnamon sugar. Bake for 10–12 minutes. Leave to cool on a wire rack. Once cool, paint the inside of the cake pan liberally with melted butter and place the pan on a baking sheet.

Increase the oven temperature to 220°C (430°F) Gas 9.

For the filling, make sure all the ingredients are at room temperature before you begin. Beat the Philadelphia cream cheese until creamy, before gradually adding the sugar, cornflour/cornstarch and salt. Add the vanilla seeds, lemon zest and juice, before whisking in the eggs and yolk, one at a time. Whisk in the soured cream and pour the mixture over the snickerdoodle base. Bake for 10 minutes.

Reduce the oven temperature to 110°C (230°F) Gas ¼.

Bake for a further 25 minutes. If you gently shake the pan, there should be a slight wobble in the middle. Turn the oven off and leave the cheesecake to cool in the oven for 2 hours with the oven door slightly ajar.

Spread the soured cream topping over the top of the cheesecake, right to the edges. Cover loosely with foil (without touching the top) and pop it in the fridge to set for 8 hours.

Place the pan on top of an upturned bowl and gently pull the sides of the pan down to release it, before prising the pan base off the cheesecake with a palette knife, while sliding it onto a serving plate.

For the sticky toffee cake

200 g/1⅓ cups pitted Medjool dates, chopped

240 ml/1 cup of fairly weak black tea

100 g/6½ tablespoons unsalted butter

100 g/½ cup light muscovado sugar

25 g/2 tablespoon dark muscovado

1 tablespoon golden/light corn syrup

2 large eggs, beaten

2 teaspoons mixed/apple pie spice

2 teaspoons pure vanilla extract

175 g/1⅓ cups self-raising/rising flour

1 teaspoon bicarbonate of/baking soda

Sticky Toffee Sauce (page 9)

For the banana cake

2 bananas

a squeeze of fresh lemon juice

100 g/½ cup caster/granulated sugar

100 g/6½ tablespoons soft unsalted butter

2 large eggs

a generous splash of vanilla extract

25 g/2½ tablespoons ground almonds

100 g/¾ cup self raising/rising flour

½ teaspoon baking powder

1 tablespoon demerara sugar

To assemble

Sticky Toffee Buttercream (page 9)

Vanilla Cream Cheese Topping (page 8)

dark/bittersweet chocolate, to serve

2 x 20-cm/8-inch square baking pans, greased and lined with baking parchment

a piping bag fitted with a small, round nozzle/tip

Serves 12

Just like a banana, I've mashed the flavours of the classic Banoffee Pie into a cake. A toffee cake base layer soaked with sticky toffee sauce and sandwiched with a light and fluffy banana sponge cake.

Banoffee cake

Preheat the oven to 180°C (350°F) Gas 4.

To make the sticky toffee cake, put the dates and tea in a saucepan or pot set over a medium heat. Allow to boil for about 5 minutes, then take the pan off the heat and reserve for later. Cream the butter and sugars together until pale and fluffy. Gradually add the egg, whisking between each addition. Add the golden/light corn syrup, vanilla extract, mixed/apple pie spice and date and tea mixture and mix well. Sift over the flour and bicarbonate of/baking soda and fold in until thoroughly combined.

Pour the mixture into one of the prepared cake pans and bake for around 45 minutes or until an inserted skewer comes out clean. Remove from the oven but leave the oven on for the banana cake.

Place the sticky toffee cake, still in its pan, on a wire rack and stab all over with a skewer, before pouring over a few tablespoons of hot sticky toffee sauce (see page 9). Once the cake has been drizzled, allow the sauce to cool before using it to make the sticky toffee buttercream (see page 9).

To make the banana cake, slice one of the bananas, place in a bowl and squeeze over the lemon juice to prevent the banana from browning. Reserve for later. Mash the other banana and place in a mixing bowl with the butter, sugar, eggs, vanilla extract and ground almonds. Sift over the flour and baking powder and whisk the ingredients together for a couple of minutes until well combined, pale and fluffy. Add some milk to slacken the mixture if necessary and whisk again.

Pour the cake mixture into the prepared pan and smooth over the top. Place the sliced banana over the top of the cake in concentric circles, sprinkle over the demerara sugar and place in the oven for 25–30 minutes, or until an inserted skewer comes out clean. If the bananas on top start to catch, place a sheet of parchment paper over the top of the cake for the remaining cooking time.

Once baked, place the cake, still in its pan, on a wire rack to cool completely before turning out.

To assemble, place the sticky toffee cake on a serving plate and spread the sticky toffee buttercream over the top. Spread a generous helping of sticky toffee sauce on top. Place the banana cake, sliced banana side up, on top. Spoon the vanilla cream cheese topping into a piping bag and pipe small peaks of cream over the top of the cake. Grate over some dark/bittersweet chocolate and serve.

A stack of crepes filled with rich chocolate crème pâtissière and sliced in wedges make this cake the perfect Pancake Day treat. But once you've tried crake, you'll wish it was Shrove Tuesday every day.

Crake

For the crepe batter
100 g/6½ tablespoons unsalted butter

6 eggs

200 g/1⅔ cups plain/all-purpose flour, sifted

a pinch of salt

100 g/½ cup caster/granulated sugar

750 ml/3 cups whole milk, warmed in a pan

2 teaspoons pure vanilla extract

For the chocolate crème pâtissière
6 egg yolks

90 g/scant ½ cup caster/granulated sugar

30 g/¼ cup cornflour/cornstarch

1 tablespoon unsweetened cocoa powder

a pinch of salt

525 ml/2¼ cups whole milk

1 vanilla pod/bean, split lengthwise and seeds scraped out

unsweetened cocoa powder, to dust

Serves 8

To make the crepe batter, melt the butter in a small pan until golden brown and nutty. Whisk together the eggs, flour, sugar, and salt into a large jug/pitcher. Slowly add the warm milk, browned butter and vanilla extract. Cover the jug/pitcher with clingfilm/plastic wrap and put in the fridge for several hours or overnight.

To make the crème pâtissière, place the egg yolks and sugar in a heatproof bowl and whisk until pale and fluffy. Sift over the cornflour/cornstarch and cocoa and whisk in. Place the milk and vanilla in a saucepan or pot set over a gentle heat and bring up to a simmer. Fish out the vanilla pod and slowly pour the milk over the eggs, whisking as you do so. Decant the custard back into the pan and stir over a medium heat and bring to the boil. Once the custard is thick enough to dollop, pour it into a cold bowl or jug/pitcher and cover the top with clingfilm/plastic wrap to prevent a skin forming. Leave to cool to room temperature before putting it in the fridge.

Next, make the crepes. Bring the batter up to room temperature. Lightly oil a non-stick crepe/pancake pan and place over a medium heat. Swirl about 3 ladles of crepe batter to cover the surface of the pan and cook until the bottom of the crepe becomes lightly browned. Flip the crepe and lightly cook the other side. Place the cooked crepe onto a piece of baking parchment and repeat this process until you have about 20 crepes. Do not stack the crepes on top of each other to cool, or they will become soggy. Leave to cool.

Place one crepe on a serving plate and spread over a spoonful of crème pâtissière evenly before placing another crepe on top. Repeat this process until all the crepes are stacked. Spread a final layer of crème pâtissière on the top crepe and refrigerate for at least 3 hours to set. Dust liberally with cocoa powder to serve.

For the flapjack crust

300 g/1½ cups light muscovado sugar
300 g/2½ sticks soft, unsalted butter
4 tablespoons golden/light corn syrup
400 g/3 cups rolled porridge oats
½ teaspoon salt

For the mud cake

35 g/1 oz. dark/bittersweet chocolate, broken into pieces
75 g/⅓ cup dark muscovado sugar
65 ml/¼ cup whole milk
25 g/2 tablespoons butter, softened
1 large egg, beaten
a splash of pure vanilla extract
a pinch of salt
10 g/1½ tablespoons unsweetened cocoa
40 g/⅓ cup plain/all-purpose flour
½ teaspoon bicarbonate of/baking soda

For the mud mousse

225 g/8 oz. dark/bittersweet chocolate, broken into pieces
150 g/10 tablespoons unsalted butter
5 eggs, separated
85 g/⅔ cup icing/confectioners' sugar
a pinch of salt
135 ml/½ cup double/heavy cream

To decorate

Sweet Cream Topping (page 8)
50 g/1½ oz. dark/bittersweet chocolate shavings (optional)

a 20-cm/8-inch springform cake pan, greased and lined with baking parchment

Serves 12

Mississippi Mud Pie gets a makeover with an oaty flapjack base. Rich, decadent and sticky, it's hard to stop at just one slice.

Mississippi mud jack

Preheat the oven to 150°C (300°F) Gas 2.

To make the flapjack crust, melt the sugar, butter and golden/light corn syrup together over a gentle heat, stirring all the time. Take the pan off the heat and stir in the porridge oats and salt until fully combined and coated. Spoon the flapjack mixture into the prepared cake pan and press it down into the base and up the sides with the back of a spoon. You can push the flapjack base further up the insides of the cake pan for a more delicate finish. Bake in the preheated oven for 25 minutes. Leave to cool in the pan on top of a wire rack.

While the base cools, prepare the mud cake mixture. Preheat the oven to 180°C (350°F) Gas 4. Place the chocolate, 25 g/2 tablespoons of the sugar and the milk in a saucepan or pot set over a low heat. Stir until the sugar and chocolate have melted. Allow to cool slightly. Cream the butter with the remaining sugar in a separate bowl. Gradually whisk in the eggs and stir in the vanilla and salt. Whisk in the melted chocolate, sugar and milk. Sift over the dry ingredients and fold in. Pour the batter onto your cooled flapjack crust and bake for 15–20 minutes, or until an inserted skewer comes out clean. Place the cake pan on top of a wire rack to cool completely.

Meanwhile make the mud mousse. Melt the chocolate in a heatproof bowl suspended over a pan of barely simmering water. Once melted, take the chocolate off the heat and stir in the butter until melted. Whisk in the egg yolks, one at a time, until fully incorporated. Sift over the icing sugar and mix in. In a spotlessly clean bowl and with clean whisks, whisk the egg whites with the salt to stiff peaks. Set aside while you whisk the cream to stiff peaks – there's no need to wash up the whisks for the cream. Fold the cream into the chocolate mixture. Next, fold in the egg whites using a large metal spoon. Pour the mousse over the top of the cold mud cake and pop it in the fridge to cool for at least 8 hours (or overnight).

Once the mousse has set, run a palette knife around the inside edges of the cake pan to release the cake. Use a palette knife to carefully lever the flapjack crust off the base and slide it onto a serving plate.

Whisk the cream until stiff but not dry. Sift over the icing/confectioners' sugar and mix in. Add the vanilla and whisk again. Spread the cream in billowing peaks over the top of the mud mousse. Scatter the chocolate shavings over the top of the cream to decorate, and serve in slices.

Bring campfire fun into your sundae glass with this deliciously decadent mash-up. Homemade marshmallows, chocolate and cookies with a touch of cinnamon all smooshed into creamy vanilla ice cream.

S'more sundae

For the cookies

125 g/1 cup plain/all-purpose flour

60 g/½ cup wholemeal/whole-wheat flour

85 g/scant ½ cup dark brown sugar

½ teaspoon bicarbonate of/baking soda

¼ teaspoon salt

100 g/6½ tablespoons cold unsalted butter, cut into cubes

55 g/¼ cup runny honey

40 ml/2 tablespoons plus 2 teaspoons milk

2 teaspoons pure vanilla extract

1 tablespoon caster/superfine sugar, for the topping

1 teaspoon ground cinnamon, for the topping

For the ice cream

4 egg yolks

100 g/½ cup caster/granulated sugar

350 ml/1½ cups single/light cream

1 vanilla pod/bean

To assemble

Marshmallows (page 9)

Chocolate Fudge Sauce (page 8)

50 g/1½ oz. dark/bittersweet chocolate, broken into pieces

2 x baking sheets, greased and lined with baking parchment

Makes 5

To make the cookies, place the flours, brown sugar, bicarbonate of/baking soda and salt in a food processor and blitz to incorporate. Add the butter and pulse until the mixture is the consistency of breadcrumbs. Add the honey, milk and vanilla and pulse again until the mixture forms a ball of dough. Wrap the dough in clingfilm/plastic wrap and put it in the fridge for at least 2 hours.

Roll the dough out onto a lightly floured work surface into a long rectangle about 3 mm/1/12 inch thick. Trim the edges and cut the dough into 10 even-sized rectangles. Mix the sugar and cinnamon together in a bowl to make the topping. Put the rectangles on the baking sheets and sprinkle with the topping. Pop back in the fridge to firm up for at least 30 minutes.

Preheat the oven to 180°C (350°F) Gas 4. Bake for 15–20 minutes, until golden and slightly firm to the touch. Transfer to a wire rack to cool.

To make the ice cream, whisk the egg yolks and sugar together in a large heatproof bowl until pale and thickened. Split the vanilla pods/bean lengthwise and scrape out the seeds. Put the cream and vanilla pods/beans and seeds into a large saucepan or pot set over a gentle heat. When the mixture just begins to boil, remove from the heat, pour over the egg mixture through a sieve/strainer and whisk thoroughly (discard the vanilla pods/beans). Return the custard to the pan and place over a gentle heat. Stir continuously until the custard is thick enough to coat the back of a spoon and pour into a cold jug/pitcher. Break up a third of the cookies and fold them through the custard along with half of the marshmallows (see page 9), chopped into small pieces. Put a sheet of clingfilm/plastic wrap over the top to prevent a skin forming and leave to cool. Put in the fridge for 1 hour. Then put the custard into a freezer-proof, plastic container and put it in the freezer. Whisk vigorously every 30 minutes to prevent ice crystals forming. The ice cream should be completely set within 3–4 hours.

Preheat the oven to 180°C (350°F) Gas 4.

Place the cookies on a baking sheet. Place the broken chocolate pieces on top of each one and bake for a few minutes, or until the chocolate has melted. In the meantime, use a blowtorch to brown the marshmallows to give them a smoky, campfire flavour. Sandwich them inbetween the cookies. Then layer up scoops of ice cream and chocolate fudge sauce and top each sundae with a S'more.

For the cake

150 g/5 oz. dark/bittersweet
chocolate, broken into pieces

5 eggs, separated

150 g/¾ cup caster/granulated sugar

1 tablespoon unsweetened cocoa
powder

a pinch of salt

For the chocolate custard

6 egg yolks

100 g/½ cup caster/granulated sugar

1 tablespoon cornflour/cornstarch

500 ml/2 cups double/heavy cream

1 vanilla pod/bean, split in half
lengthwise and seeds scraped out

100 g/3½ oz. dark/bittersweet
chocolate, broken into pieces

1 tablespoon kirsch

To assemble

500 g/16 oz. kirsch soaked cherries
(drained weight)

115 ml/½ cup kirsch

3 tablespoons Morello cherry jam/
jelly

300 ml/1¼ cups double/whipping
cream

1 tablespoon icing/confectioners'
sugar, sifted

30 g/1 oz. grated dark/bittersweet
chocolate, grated

fresh cherries, to decorate (optional)

*a 20-cm/8-inch round cake pan,
greased and lined with baking
parchment*

*a 22-cm/8.5-inch round glass trifle dish,
10 cm/4-inches deep*

Serves 8-10

Black Forest Trifle, a hybrid of the classic Black Forest Gateau crossed with a trifle, has everything you want from a dessert. Rich, silky and studded with booze-soaked cherries, the B. F. T. is a real treat!

The B. F. T.

Preheat the oven to 180°C (350°F) Gas 4.

Melt the chocolate in a heatproof bowl suspended over a pan of barely simmering water. Once melted, take the bowl off the heat and leave to cool slightly. Put the egg whites and salt in a large bowl and whisk to stiff peaks. In a separate bowl, whisk the egg yolks and sugar together until pale and mousse-like. Whisk in the cooled melted chocolate before beating in one third of the stiff egg white. Fold the remaining egg whites into the chocolate mixture with a large metal spoon, until fully combined. Sift over the cocoa and fold through carefully until there are no remaining streaks in the batter. Be careful not to knock the air out of the mixture. Pour the mixture into the prepared pan and bake for 20–25 minutes, or until an inserted skewer comes out clean. Leave the cake to cool in the pan for 10 minutes, before turning out on a wire rack to cool completely.

To make the custard, melt the chocolate in a heatproof bowl suspended over a pan of barely simmering water. Once melted, take the bowl off the heat and leave to cool slightly. Whisk the egg yolks, cornflour/cornstarch and sugar together in a large heatproof bowl until pale and thickened and place a sieve/strainer over the top. Split the vanilla pod/bean in half lengthwise and scrape out the seeds. Place the cream and vanilla pods/beans and seeds into a large saucepan or pot set over a gentle heat. When the mixture just begins to boil pour over the egg mixture through the sieve/strainer and whisk thoroughly. Return the custard to the pan and place over a gentle heat. Stir continuously until the custard has thickened and pour into a cold jug/pitcher to prevent it from cooking any further. Stir the melted chocolate and kirsch into the custard until fully combined and streak free. Cover the jug/pitcher with clingfilm/plastic wrap to prevent a skin forming. Once cold, transfer the custard to the fridge to chill.

Push the cooled cake into the bottom of a trifle dish. Splash the kirsch over the top of the cake and scatter over the cherries. Spoon the custard on top of the cherries and smooth over the top with a palette knife. Whisk the cream and icing/confectioners' sugar together until stiff but not dry and spread over the top of the custard. Decorate with the grated chocolate and fresh cherries (if using) and return to the fridge until ready to serve.

A fruit cobbler crossed with a waffle, a wobbler is comfort food at its best. Soft, sweet plums with a crisp waffle topping, this makes a delicious, warming dessert – perfect served with a dollop of vanilla ice cream or a generous pouring of hot vanilla custard. This recipe will also be delicious with other fruits.

Wobbler

For the waffles

250 g/2 cups plain/all-purpose flour

30 g/2½ tablespoons caster/granulated sugar

2 teaspoons baking powder

¼ teaspoon salt

2 eggs, separated

125 g/1 stick unsalted butter, melted

435 ml/1¾ cups whole milk

1 teaspoon pure vanilla extract

1 tablespoon caster/granulated sugar, to sprinkle

1 teaspoon ground cinnamon, to sprinkle

For the plums

12 plums, pitted and cut in quarters

50 g/¼ cup light muscovado sugar

2 teaspoons pure vanilla extract

50 g/3 tablespoons unsalted butter, softened

a waffle iron

Serves 6

Preheat the waffle iron.

To make the waffles, stir the flour, sugar and baking powder together in a large mixing bowl. Add the egg yolks, melted butter, milk and vanilla extract and lightly whisk together until fully incorporated. Don't over-mix the ingredients though, or your waffles will be heavy.

In another bowl, whisk the egg whites with the salt until stiff but not dry. Fold the egg whites into the batter with a large metal spoon.

Spray the preheated waffle iron with non-stick cooking spray. Ladle the mixture into the hot waffle iron and bake for 2–3 minutes until golden brown. Mix together the caster/granulated sugar and cinnamon and sprinkle a little over each waffle while they're still hot. Set aside.

Preheat the oven to 180°C (350°F) Gas 4.

Arrange the plums in an even layer in an ovenproof dish. Sprinkle over the light muscovado sugar and vanilla extract. Break off little pieces of butter and scatter them over the plums. Place the waffles over the top of the plums and place a sheet of baking parchment followed by a sheet of foil over the top. Bake for 20 minutes before removing the parchment and foil and popping the dish back in the oven to bake for a further 10 minutes, or until the waffles are golden brown with a few crispy edges. Serve hot with pouring cream or vanilla ice cream.

Index

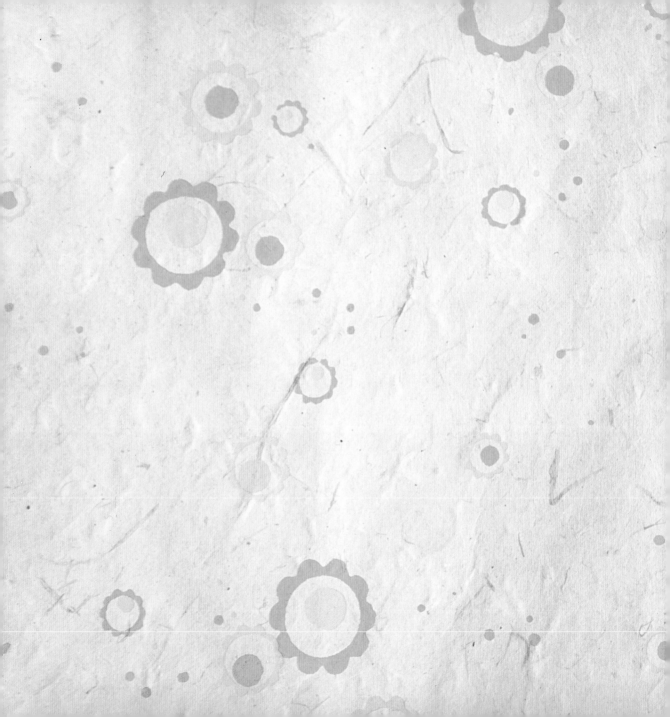